32 Sugar Free Holiday Cookie Recipes

D1522426

ANNIE BUSCO
THE SUGAR FREE DIVA

Annie Busco

The Sugar Free Diva

1st Edition

Acknowledgments

This book could not have been written without the support of my wonderful readers.

I would like to take this opportunity to thank all of the wonderful people who have religiously stopped by thesugarfreediva.com to see the recipes that I have shared. Many of these people have given me praise for the delicious results that they have had. Often, my readers have also given me advice, suggestions, adjustment ideas. and other helpful feedback.

Also, I would also like to thank my good friends who have listened to my thoughts and ideas. They have been supportive, encouraging, as well as realistic with me when needed.

Lastly, I have been extremely blessed with a wonderful and loving family who are the benefactors of my creations as well as the people who have had to step aside while I have created this book. Certainly, my four legged family members are quite important as well.

Thank you for purchasing this book as well as my other books. I appreciate your support!

About This Book

This book has been a long time coming.

For many of us, our first adventure into the world of sugar free baking is in the form of cookie baking. We want to enjoy our cookies but, really must or choose to avoid the sugar that often makes those cookies taste so good.

Perhaps you ventured into the world of sugar free baking for someone else. While you are not sensitive to sugar, someone that you care for is so you are baking something that they too can enjoy.

Whether you are baking without sugar for yourself or for others, you are here for a reason. That reason is to make cookies that taste great yet, do not have a lot of added sugar in them.

There are a few things that you should know about baking with sugar alternatives.

Sugar alternatives are most often used to make the food that they are added to more palatable. Would you eat a cake or candy bar that did not have some sort of sweet taste in it? You probably would not as it would taste not so great.

What you should know that there is a chemical difference between sugar and all sugar alternatives. This chemical difference can have an effect on the results of what ever you are creating. If you would like to learn about the specifics about baking with sugar alternatives, please check out my book The Sugar Free Baking Guide. This guide goes into depth about how and when to use the specific alternatives as well as the many available alternatives that you can use.

What is important to know is that not every sugar alternative is suitable for every recipe. This is not only for taste but, for the chemical build of that alternative and its ability to be used in that recipe as a result.

The choice of which sugar alternative to use is up to you. I will tell you in each recipe which kind of sugar alternative works best in that recipe. For example, if you see 'granular sugar alternative' that usually means that there is a volume of dry ingredient factor to take into consideration, and thus, using a liquid alternative will not work in that recipe as it is written.

Reading the label on the package of the sugar alternative is just as essential to making a successful recipe. On that label look for the equivalence of that product to sugar. What I mean is that look to see if one cup of that product equivalent in volume to 1 cup of sugar.

Also worth noting on the label is exactly what is in that product. Often there can be a blend of products to get to that 1:1 volume equivalence to sugar. Sometimes there could be sugar used to get that volume equivalence.

Not all sugar alternatives are sugar free. I am talking about natural products such as honey. This means that you are perhaps getting a 'healthier' alternative to processed sugar in a natural sugar form. For some people it is not as much about sugar free as it is about being naturally sweetened.

The world of sugar alternatives has evolved since I have started using them in recipes. This really is an ongoing thing as well as I seem to notice new ideas and products all of the time. You can see why it would be so important to read those product labels even more as a result.

Sometimes a recipe will call for an ingredient that will come with its own sugar alternative. Most specifically I have seen this when it comes to cookies is the chocolate chip. Many chocolate chips will be sweetened with sugar alternatives that may not be friendly to the intestines when consumed in certain amounts. This is something that you may want to be aware of.

So what sugar alternative is best for you to use?
What I can tell you is that there are lab created alternatives that are usually less expensive and seem to be promoted well by their manufacturers. These alternatives seem to cost less than the more natural products and are more popular as a results.

On the other hand, the more natural products, sugar alternatives that we can trace to plants, are popular because folks say that they are less unhealthy than the lab created alternatives because they are natural. These sugar alternatives are usually more expensive yet, more likely to be blended because less of these alternatives are needed to achieve the same level of sweetness as sugar has in a recipe.

Choosing a sugar alternative can be confusing but, you will most likely find what works best for you before you know it. Like anything else, you can expect there to be some trial and error involved when it comes to baking sugar free. Learning how to read the product labels on the alternative is essential as you will find out if you have not already.

This book is a compilation of both new cookie recipes and some of the most popular cookie recipe from TheSugarFreeDiva.com

Lastly, there is a webpage address listed after each of the recipes.

Please refer to that specific webpage when searching for further details including ingredient information. I usually provide alternatives such as gluten free ingredients or vegan ingredients in the recipes in this book. I also provide extra tips as do my readers in the comment section.

Why We Choose To Use Alternatives To Sugar

Let me start by telling you why I bake with sugar alternatives.

I would have to first admit that I am a recovering sugar addict. While this may seem kind of funny or cute, it is real. I was (am) addicted to sugar.

My addiction started as a child when it seems as if everything had sugar in it. Every suburban mother, like mine, was encouraged to serve their kids sugared beverages, sugared treats, and sugared everything else. There were no options available without sugar in them and as a result, kids gained weight and dental bills got big. As a child, once I ate my piece of fruit per day, sugar was my best friend. I lived for that sweetness like nothing else.

It was not until I was an adult that I realized that sugar controlled me rather than I controlled it. The more sugar I ate, the more sugar I craved. It became a vicious sugar cycle that I needed to gain control over. Learning how to use alternative in my kitchen creations helped me gain that control

The struggle with sugar is real for a lot of us. Check out this research to see what I mean.

Before there were grocery stores with prepared food (over 100 years ago basically), American's consumed about two pounds of sugar in a year. Two pounds is about 192 teaspoons which would mean that Americans consumed about half a teaspoon of sugar in a day. Wow!

50 years ago (about the time of the onset of suburbia and grocery stores) that amount of consumed sugar jumped up to over 120

pounds of sugar in a year. 11,520 teaspoons or 31 1/2 teaspoons of sugar per day.

Today Americans have decreased their consumption of sugar to as much around 20 teaspoons of sugar daily (according to the AHA). This can be attributed to education and smart consumer choices which have made an impact on sugar consumption.

Clearly, I am not the only person giving up sugar.
I gave up sugar because I did not like what I call the 'Sugar Rollercoaster". The roller coaster of the sugar high that is followed to the sugar low. One minute I have a lot of energy and a short while later I need a nap.

It is not just the sugar roller coaster that turned me into a sugar free person. Sugar consumption took its toll on my weight as well as my teeth. In the end, I always felt controlled by sugar rather than me controlling the sugar.

Yes, there are a lot of choices of sugar alternatives that you can theoretically use in a recipe.

Our goal in using sugar alternatives in recipes is achieving a sweetness like that of sugar in a recipe. However, you should know that not all sugar alternatives are meant to be baked or cooked with due to their chemical makeup.

If you would like to learn more about sugar alternatives and how to use them, you can check out my book The Sugar Free Baking

Guide on Amazon. I go into more depth about the many alternatives out there including the natural ones.

I prefer using a granular sugar alternative in most of my cookie recipes.

You will see 'granular' in the ingredient listing to let you know that I suggest that you should be using a granular alternative in that recipe as well. This is because a granular sugar alternative is more like sugar when it comes to the dry ingredient volume in a recipe. There are plenty of granular choices for you to choose from which include the natural and artificial ones.

When I first started baking with sugar alternatives there were few sugar free alternative choices for brown sugar. You either had to use a white sugar alternative instead or actually use the brown sugar itself. Today there are alternatives, albeit not a lot, however there are alternatives for brown sugar, which can be a good thing for chocolate chip cookies everywhere.

Again, I will mention that if you need help finding a product or alternative, such as for brown sugar, please refer to the web address at the end of each recipe in this book.

Factors That Can Affect Your Cookie Results.

Obviously, since we are not using the same sugar that is used in regular cookies, there will be some difference in the cookies that we bake.

The biggest difference between sugared cookies and sugar alternatives cookies is in the sweet taste of the cookies. Sugar alternative cookies may taste sweet thanks to the sugar alternatives that are used to replace sugar but, the cookies will not taste 100% like the regular cookies. They may also have some kind of an after taste or other aftereffect thanks to that alternative. But, at least you are not using sugar.

Sugar in cookies does more than just sweeten up cookies.

Sugar has other roles besides sweetening a recipe. It also helps hold on to the moisture that other ingredients that are added to a mixing bowl. While we can make adjustments for this in a recipe, it is still possible that your cookies will end up a bit more dry than the regular cookies with sugar in them

Summing up the role of sugar, it is added to recipes to make baked foods taste sweeter. Sugar is also added to help maintain the volume of the dry ingredients to the wet ingredients as well as hold on to moisture in what we bake.

Another factor that can affect how your cookies turn out can be the weather. If it is dry where you are then your recipe can come out a bit dry. On the flip side, if it is moist in your location then your recipe may hold on to moisture better.

There are a few steps that you can take to enhance your sugar free cookie baking results.

First off, use fresh ingredients. This is especially true when it comes to leveling agents.

Also Important to the success of your cookie baking is using granular sugar alternatives rather than the forms of alternatives. I have already mentioned that the granular sugar alternatives that you use should be measured 1:1 with sugar in recipes for best results. You can refer to the label on the package to see how your sugar alternative measures with sugar when used in recipes.

Lastly, follow the instructions step by step. I give step by step instructions in a certain order because ingredients often have their own personalities and in order to get along with the other ingredients, they may need to be introduced to the batter in a certain way or method.

I have also mentioned that there is a web page address following each individual recipe which will take you to the actual published recipe. Referring to that address will help you find ingredients, explain the ingredients and recipe in further details and may offer you ingredient alternatives that can work in that recipe.

I almost always offer special diet alternatives in those recipes. The special diets may include keto, vegan, or gluten free diets.

About The Ingredients Used In Sugar Free Baking

I have been experimenting in my kitchen with alternatives to sugar for most of my life. As expected, some experiments turned out better than others.

While this may seem to be redundant, I thing is important to mention again. Some folks, like myself sometimes, like to not always read a book such as this one in the order of chapters. As a result, you may have skipped over this.

What you need to keep in mind about baking with sugar alternatives is that not all sugar alternatives are the same. While sugar alternatives may add the sweetness that is lost when we take sugar out of a recipe, alternatives are not chemically the same as sugar. As a result of this chemical difference , sugar alternatives usually behave differently than sugar when used in recipes.

This is especially true when they are exposed to factors such as heat. For example, sugar alternatives containing aspartame do not chemically bake well. If you use aspartame then your cookie results will suffer. The good news is that there are many other granular alternatives available for baking these days.

The recipes in this book will come with sugar alternative suggestions, I suggest the kind of sugar alternative that would work best in that recipe. For example, using a granular sugar alternative that is measured the same as you would measure sugar (1:1), should not disrupt the volume of dry ingredients in a recipe like other sugar alternatives could.

You probably have noticed the trend these days of natural alternatives to sugar. An example of a natural sugar alternative would be sugar alternatives that are made with the Stevia.

Here is what you need to know about the Stevia sweetened alternatives. Because Stevia is so much sweeter than sugar is, less of it is needed in a recipe than sugar would be needed to achieve the same level of sweetness. To keep the dry volume of the entire product equivalent to sugar, many Stevia sweeteners are mixed with other ingredients to 'bulk' them up. Often, Stevia will be mixed with sugar.

Another popular sugar alternative ingredient is Sucralose. Sucralose is perhaps the most common sugar alternative used in recipes. Not only has it been around for a while, Sucralose is a lot like sugar when it is baked (with a few adjustments here and there with many recipes). Also, it is usually less expensive than most of the other alternatives.

You will notice in my recipes that I do not mention a certain name or brand of sugar alternative to use. I simply may suggest which kind to use for the success of a recipe. You can use the sugar alternative of your choice.

To choose the sugar alternative that would work best for you in your recipe, I may suggest a sugar alternative that is best for the success of the recipe. I also suggest to choose an alternative that is best for you and your body as some alternatives may not be for you.

As a word of caution, or reminder, many sugar alternatives should be eaten in moderation, as suggested by the manufacturers and experts. Please read the label on the packaging of your chosen sugar alternatives to learn more.

While we are on the topic, my biggest piece of advice that I could give you is to read the label on the sugar alternative packaging. Look for the ingredient label to see if there has been anything added to 'bulk up' the package. Also, look for how much of the product equals one cup of sugar in a recipe (is it 1:1 with sugar?). Lastly, look to see if that alternative will work for your kind of a recipe (especially if baking with it) and any warnings associated with the product.

1: The Best Sugar Free Chocolate Chip Cookies

I titled this recipe "The Best' in because it has been a very popular chocolate chip cookie recipe with my readers. The name of this recipe is also inspired by a more famous chocolate chip cookie recipe that you may have tried in the past.

To make this recipe you should use a granular sugar alternative that measures 1:1 with regular sugar in order to keep your ingredient volume intact. You could also make this chocolate chip cookie low in carbs or gluten free by using other substitutions.

Refer to the webpage following this recipe for alternative ingredients. Make this chocolate chip cookie recipe gluten free by using gluten free flour instead of regular flour. Or, you can make this recipe low carb by using low carb flour. Lastly, you can make this 'keto friendly' by using a keto friendly flour.

What You Will Need To Make This Chocolate Chip Cookie Recipe.

Flour– 2 1/4 cups.
Baking Soda– 1 teaspoon.
Butter- 1 cup + 1 tablespoon. The is 17 tablespoons or two sticks plus a tablespoon. Have your butter softened to room temperature to make it easier to work with as well.
Granular White Sugar Alternative – 1 cup. Use a sugar alternative that measures 1:1 with sugar for best results.
Brown Sugar Alternative – 1/2 cup. Use granular that measures 1:1 with sugar in volume.
Eggs- 2.
Vanilla Extract– 1 teaspoon.

Sugar Free Chocolate Chips– 1 bag. Most bags are 8-9 ounces in volume.

How To Make The Best Sugar Free Chocolate Chip Cookies

- *Start by preheating your oven to 350 and prepping a cookie sheet for nonstick (I use parchment paper for an easy clean up).*
- *In a medium sized bowl, whisk together the flour and baking soda. Set this bowl aside.*
- *Next, in a mixing bowl, cream together the butter and the sugars. I use a paddle attachment and scrape the sides of the bowl as needed.*
- *For the next step we are going to add the dry ingredients from the first bowl to the ingredients in the second bowl. To do so, add half of the dry ingredients to the mixing bowl, stir gently and then add the remaining ingredients and stir gently again. Then add the eggs and the vanilla extract.*
- *Lastly, fold in the chocolate chips.*
- *Bake your cookies for 10-12 minutes or until they begin to brown. Larger cookies will most likely take longer than smaller cookies to bake. Also, some folks prefer their cookies baked longer than others.*

Read more at: https://thesugarfreediva.com/sugar-free-chocolate-chip-cookies/

2: Soft And Chewy Sugar Free Chocolate Chip Cookies

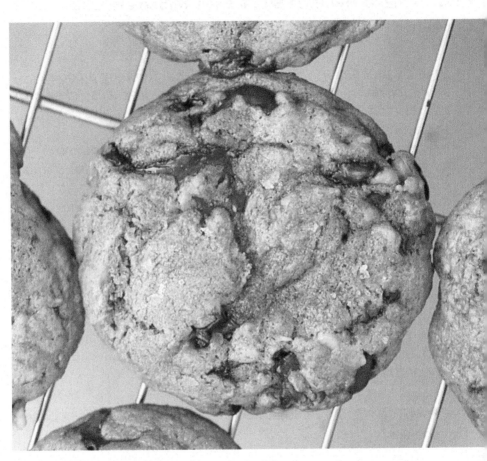

Sometimes you just need a soft chocolate chip cookie. That soft cookie is a visual reminder of both a warm cookie just out of the oven and the scent that comes with that cookie. ahhhh!

The secret to making a softer cookie is molasses. Molasses helps the cookie hold on to the moisture that it needs to stay soft. However, molasses also contains sugar, even though it may often be considered to be friendly to some low sugar diets. I do have a few workarounds for the molasses though that I will share with you in this recipe.

As mentioned with other cookie recipes, you may need a flour alternative depending on your diet. Make this recipe gluten free by using gluten free flour instead of regular flour. Or, you can make this recipe low carb by using low carb flour. Also, you will need sugar free chocolate chips, as well as a brown sugar alternative (sugar free).

What you will need to make Soft and Chewy Chocolate Chip Cookies.

Flour- 2 cups
Baking Powder- 1/2 teaspoon.
Salt- 1/2 teaspoon (feel free to omit if using margarine that has salt in it).
Margarine or shortening-1 cup melted or really really soft (depending on what works best with what you are using).
Granular Sugar Alternative- 1 cup 1:1 equivalent to sugar.
Brown Sugar Alternative– 1/2 cup.
Vanilla Extract- 1 teaspoon.
Egg-1.
Egg Yolks- 2
Sugar Free Chocolate Chips– 1 cup, room temperature.

How To Make Soft And Chewy Sugar Free Chocolate Chip Cookies.

- *It is best to use a new or newer cookie sheet (one that has not blackened or changed color at all. Prep this cookie sheet with parchment paper. Preheat your oven to 325.*
- *In a medium sized bowl, stir together the flour (or alternative), baking powder, and salt. Set this aside.*
- *Now in a large mixing bowl, stir together the margarine (or alternative) and the sugars. This recipe actually works even better by mixing by hand rather than using an electric mixer, although you could use on if needed.*
- *Next, stir in the vanilla extract and the eggs/egg yolks (on egg or yolk at a time).*
- *Add the dry ingredients from the medium mixing bowl to the large mixing bowl and blend.*
- *Lastly, fold in the chocolate chips.*
- *Bake these for 12-15 minutes or until the edges begin to brown.*
- *Allow the cookies to cool at room temperature on the baking sheet. Immediately store in an air tight container (adding a slice of bread will help keep them moist.)Note that some people like to make these cookies extra large. That could result in the cookies needed a bit of extra time to bake in the oven.*

Read more at: https://thesugarfreediva.com/soft-and-chewy-sugar-free-chocolate-chip-cookies/

3: Sugar Free Peanut Butter Chocolate Chip Cookies

I like the idea of combining two great cookies into one. Certainly, peanut butter cookies and chocolate chip cookies are good choices for many of us too.

To keep these cookies as low as possible in sugar, we will need to use a sugar free peanut butter. I have a recipe for sugar free peanut butter r on the sugarfreediva.com or you can purchase sugar free peanut butter. I suggest looking for organic peanut butter if you have trouble finding the sugar free peanut butter. The organic peanut butter often has no added sugar in it too, but read the label to make sure.

What you need to make sugar free peanut butter chocolate chip cookies.

Flour- 1 1/2 cups
Baking Soda- 1 teaspoon.
Butter- 1 cup (2 sticks) plus 1 tablespoon. This should be softened to room temperature.
Sugar Free Peanut Butter – 1/2 cup (any texture works in this recipe). Granular Sugar Alternative- 1/2 cup. I suggest a granular sugar alternative that measures 1:1 with granular sugar.
Brown Sugar Alternative- 1/2 cup. Again, I suggest a granular brown sugar alternative that measures 1:1 with brown sugar.
Vanilla Extract- 2 teaspoons.
Egg- 1.
Semi Sweet Sugar Free Chocolate Chips– 1 eight or 9 ounce bag. I like how semi sweet chocolate chips interact with the other ingredients in a cookie. However, you can also try an unsweetened chocolate chip or a dark sugar free chocolate chip if desired.

How To Make Sugar Free Peanut Butter Chocolate Chip Cookies

- *Start by prepping a cookie sheet for nonstick (I like parchment paper) and preheating your oven to 350.*
- *In a small bowl, whisk or sift together the flour and the baking soda. Next, in a mixing bowl, beat together the butter, peanut butter, and sugars until creamy. Then add the vanilla extract and egg.*
- *Add half of the flour mixture from the first bowl to the second bowl. Mix gently and then add the rest. Then you can fold in the chocolate chips.*
- *Bake your cookies for 10 to 12 minutes or until the edges begin to brown.*

Read more at: https://thesugarfreediva.com/sugar-free-peanut-butter-chocolate-chip-cookies/

4: One Minute Sugar Free Chocolate Chip Cookie

This recipe is a 'cookie for one', mug, or single serving recipe. It is also for those of us who do not want to spend a lot of time trying to satisfy a craving. Certainly, in this instance, that craving is for a chocolate chip cookie.

It is important that you use a microwave-safe mug to make this cookie as it is made in a microwave, hence the 'one minute'. While you may think that your mug is safe for microwave use, it is always best to look on the bottom of the mug to make sure that it stated 'microwave safe' on it.

What you will need to make this one minute sugar free chocolate chip cookie

Butter- 1 tablespoon, melted.
Brown Sugar Alternative- 2 tablespoons.
Egg Yolk- 1
Vanilla Extract-1/4 teaspoon.
Almond Flour (or other similar flour) 1/4 cup.
Milk- 1/2 teaspoon.
Sugar free chocolate chips – 2 tablespoons.

How To Make One Minute Sugar Free Chocolate Chip Cookie

While this recipe calls for making it in a microwave-safe mug, you can either eat it directly out of the mug or, transfer it to a board or dish and slice into a normal cookie shape.

- *I always like to prep my mug for nonstick before I begin. This will make it easier to remove the cookie in the end.*
- *Whip together the butter and sugar alternative in the bottom of the mug that you will be making this recipe in.*
- *Next add the egg yolk and cream the ingredients together.*
- *Lastly, stir in the remaining ingredients.*
- *Optional, you can add a few chocolate chips to the top before you are ready to microwave. Microwave on high for 35-40 seconds or until done, checking on it every 10 seconds (I like to rotate the mug when I check on it),*

- *To slice the cake, gently pry the sides of the cookie away from the sides of the mug and tip over on to a flat surface to slice.*

Don't want your cookie in a mug?

Make a regular cookie by microwaving the cookie batter on a small piece of parchment paper instead of in the mug. Be sure to shape the cookie before you microwave it and monitor the cooking time as this may need to be adjusted.

Read more at: https://thesugarfreediva.com/one-minute-sugar-free-chocolate-chip-cookie/

5: Sugar Free Sugar Cookies

This recipe for Sugar Free Sugar Cookies is a sugar free version a classic cookie. That classic cookie is a favorite cookie for many of us as well.

I really like that there is a lot that you can do with a sugar cookie. Certainly, you can make them as they are and enjoy them. But, you could also cut them into fun shapes, add color to them, or even drizzle some chocolate over them

Here is what you need to make sugar free sugar cookies

*Flour- 2 3/4 Cup
Baking Soda- 1 teaspoon.
Baking Powder- 1/2 teaspoon.
Butter- 2 sticks softened to room temperature.
Granular Sugar Alternative- equivalent to 1 1/4 cups of sugar.
Egg-1 beaten.
Vanilla Extract- 1 teaspoon.
Milk -1 teaspoon.*

How To Make Sugar Free Sugar Cookies

This recipe works best if the dough is made and then refrigerated for a couple of hours. This is especially true if you plan on using cookie cutters with it. However, you could just roll these out and flatten them in order to bake immediately.

- *Start by sifting together your baking soda, baking powder and flour in a bowl. Set this aside.*
- *In a mixing bowl, creme together the butter and sugar alternative. Once the butter and sugar alternative is creamed together, add the egg, vanilla extract ,and milk and mix for about 10 seconds until somewhat mixed in.*
- *Slowly pour in half of the contents from the first bowl (flour etc), mix for a few seconds and then add the remaining contents from the first bowl.*

- *Cover the dough and refrigerate the dough for at least a couple of hours. You can skip this step if you are simply going to roll the cookies into a ball and press them flat for baking.*
- *When you are ready to bake the cookies, Preheat your oven to 350 and prep a pan for nonstick.*
- *Roll out the dough (a portion at a time works best) and cut into shapes, use a cookie press, or simply place flattened balls onto the pan.*
- *Bake these cookies for 10-12 minutes or until they begin to brown. For an option, you can sprinkle additional sugar alternative over the cookies after about 10 minutes of baking.*

Read more at: https://thesugarfreediva.com/sugar-free-sugar-cookies/

6: Sugar Free Shortbread Cookies

Sugar Free Shortbread Cookies could be my favorite holiday cookie ever. This is the cookie that I will put into my cookie press before any other cookie.

A basic shortbread cookie recipe has four to five ingredients depending on whether or not you add salt. You could also use salted butter to get some salt into the cookie. This success of this cookie rests in the butter and how soft your butter really is. I should also mention that this is an egg-free cookie. This is great news for anyone who follows an egg free diet.

Here is what you will need to make this shortbread cookie.

All Purpose (AP) Flour- 3 1/2 cups
Salt- 1/2 teaspoon (omit if using salted butter.)
Softened Butter- 3 sticks (3/4 lb).
If using salted butter, omit the salt listed in this recipe. Use 3/4 lb equivalent in vegan alternative.
Granular Sugar Alternative- 1 cup that measures equivalent to sugar
Vanilla Extract- 1 teaspoon.
Optional- melted chocolate or other option for topping cookie with.

How To Make Sugar Free Shortbread Cookies

I said this would be an easy cookie to make and I meant it. You can also make the batter ahead if time and refrigerate it for baking later. This cookie works well as is, shaped with cookie cutters, or pressed through a cookie press.

- *When ready to bake, preheat your oven to 350 and prep your cookie sheet. I use parchment paper on my pans. Obviously, you can postpone this step if you do not plan on baking these cookies immediately after making the dough for it.*
- *Start by whisking together the flour and salt in a medium bowl and set this bowl aside.*
- *In a large mixing bowl, cream together the softened butter and sugar alternative. Then stir in your vanilla extract.*
- *To the large mixing bowl, add the contents from the first bowl (the flour and salt) and mix.*
- *Once the ingredients are blended together you can refrigerate your cookie dough for later baking by wrapping it in plastic or you can proceed with the baking process.*
- *Using a cookie cutter? Refrigerated dough usually responds better for cookie cutters. I suggest rolling out the dough prior to refrigerating it to simplify things a bit.*
- *Cookie pressing will work well without refrigerating all of the dough first. Split the dough in half and refrigerate one half while you work with the other. This will prevent it from getting too soft for use.*
- *Bake for 12-15 minutes for smaller cookies and up to 18 -20 minutes for larger cookies or until the edges begin to brown. Allow the cookies to cool before topping.*

Read more at: https://thesugarfreediva.com/sugar-free-shortbread-cookies/

7: Sugar Free Vanilla Wafers

This cookie is a great alternative to that famous vanilla wafer cookie that we all know about. However, this cookie does not include all of the added sugar that the other one has in it.

Sugar free vanilla wafers are my favorite cookie to use with other recipes. My sugar free s'mores dip and my sugar free hazelnut spread are perfect examples of recipes that work well with sugar free vanilla wafers. However, you can just as easily eat these cookies as they are and enjoy eating them.

What you will need to make these sugar free vanilla wafers.

Flour (AP)- 1 1/2 cups.
Baking Powder- 1 teaspoon.
Butter- 1 stick (1/2 cup) + 1 tablespoon. Softened to room temperature.
Sugar Alternative-1 cup. Use an alternative that measures 1:1 equivalent in volume to sugar. Use a granular alternative for best results.
Egg- 1.
Vanilla Extract- 1 tablespoon.

How To Make Sugar Free Vanilla Wafers

- Preheat your oven to 325 and prep a cookie pan for nonstick. I use parchment paper.
- Sift or mix together the flour and the baking powder in a mixing bowl. Set this bowl aside.
- In a large mixing bowl, cream together the butter and the sugar alternative.
- Next, add the dry ingredients from the first bowl to the mixing bowl the the creamed butter and sugar alternative. I add a half at a time, gently stirring between additions.
- Once the ingredients in the mixing bowl are somewhat mixed, stir in the egg and then the vanilla extract to the mixing bowl.

- *Use a teaspoon or tablespoon to drop the cookies on to your prepped pan.*
- *Bake for 14-16 minutes or until the edges begin to brown.*

Read more at: https://thesugarfreediva.com/sugar-free-vanilla-wafers/

8: Sugar Free Red Velvet Cookies

Red velvet adds a nice visual addition to any holiday cookie display because of its lovely deep red color. Sometimes the cookie is topped with a glaze or a dusting of sugar, or in our case, sugar alternative.

I should also add that sugar free red velvet cookies are especially popular during the Valentine's Day season as well.

What you will need to make this Sugar Free Red Velvet Cookie Recipe

Flour (AP) 2 cups.
Baking Soda- 1/2 teaspoon.
Butter- 1 stick + 2 tablespoons (10 tablespoons). Softened to room temperature.
Brown Sugar Alternative– 1/2 cup.
Granular Sugar Alternative (white)- 1/2 cup that measures 1:1 equivalent to sugar.
Egg- 1.
Unsweetened/sugar free baking chocolate- 1 1/2 ounces (about three squares) melted. To melt, first break it up and then microwave it in a microwave safe cup or bowl for about thirty seconds, stirring as needed.
Red Food Coloring – 1 tablespoon (yep, tablespoon!)
Sour Cream- 3/4 cup (I have used Greek Yogurt).
Optional- Tip these cookies with one of these Sugar Free Cream Cheese Frosting Recipes. Or,Sugar Free Powdered Sugar.

How To Make Sugar Free Red Velvet Cookies

- *Preheat your oven to 350 and prep your cookie sheet for nonstick. I am a parchment paper person here.*
- *In a medium bowl, sift or whisk together the flour and baking soda. Set this aside.*
- *Next in a large mixing bowl, blend together the butter and the brown sugar alternative. When this has blended, you can add the white sugar alternative and beat until somewhat fluffy.*
- *To the large mixing bowl, stir in the melted chocolate, food coloring, and then the sour cream until somewhat blended.*

- *We are next going to add the contents from the first bowl (flour and baking soda) to the large mixing bowl. Do so half of the first bowl contents at a time, gently stirring between additions scraping the sides of the bowl as needed.*
- *Roll the cookies into balls and then flatten them on the prepped baking sheet.*
- *Bake these for 10-12 minutes (please note that these cookies should not harden in the oven and may even appear to be a bit underdone when they are ready, look for a 'springback effect' when poked).*
- *Allow these cookies to cool on the sheet (5-7 minutes) before transferring to rack.*
- *For best results bake these cookies one sheet at a time in order to bake in the middle of the oven for circulation.*
- *Top these as desired with sugar free powdered sugar or a glaze..*

Read more at: https://thesugarfreediva.com/sugar-free-red-velvet-cookies/

9: Sugar Free Snickerdoodle Cookies

I have always wondered who and how the name of this cookie came to be. Having said that, I must admit that the snickerdoodle is a staple to any most any holiday cookie table.

This is a cookie that relies upon cream of tarter to aid in the leavening process. When we add cream of tarter to the snickerdoodle cookie we are doing it to create a 'tangy' taste as well as making the cookie texture good for chewing (rather than crunching). Oddly enough, cream of tarter is a byproduct of making wine.

Here is what you will need to make your sugar free snickerdoodle cookie

Granular Sugar Alternative– 1 3/4 cups, divided. For best results, use a granular sugar alternative that measures 1:1 with sugar in volume. Cinnamon – 2 teaspoons of grounded cinnamon. Please be sure to use cinnamon that does not have sugar added to it .
All Purpose Flour– 2 3/4 cups. See post for alternatives
Cream of Tarter– 2 teaspoons.
Baking Soda– 1 teaspoon.
Salt- pinch.
Butter- 1/2 cup or 1 stick softened to room temperature.
Shortening- 1/2 cup.
Eggs- 2. You can find egg alternatives here.
Vanilla Extract– 1 teaspoon.

- *Preheat your oven to 375 and prep a cookie sheet for nonstick. I like to use Parchment Paper .*
- *In a small bowl, use a fork to mix together the cinnamon with 1/4 cup of the sugar alternative then set this bowl aside.*
- *Now, in a medium bowl, whisk or sift together your flour, cream of tarter, baking soda, and salt. Set this bowl aside for a moment while you continue to work.*
- *Next in a mixing bowl, cream together 1 1/2 cups of the sugar alternative with the butter, and shortening.*

- *For the next step we will add the dry ingredients from the first bowl to the creamed ingredients in the mixing bowl. To do this simply add half of the dry ingredients, gently mix, and then add the remaining and the gently mix again.*
- *Now we will add the eggs, one egg at a time, and then the vanilla extract to the mixing bowl.*
- *To form the cookies, simply roll each individual cookie into a ball and then roll that ball into the first bowl (small bowl with the cinnamon and sugar alternative) to cover the cookie. Then place the rolled cookie on to the prepped cookie sheet and repeat until all of the cookies have been formed. Be sure to leave plenty of room between cookies on the sheet as they will flatten as they bake.*
- *Bake your cookies for 10-12 minutes or until they begin to 'crack'. Allow them to cool on the sheet before transferring.*

Read more at: https://thesugarfreediva.com/sugar-free-snickerdoodle-cookies/

10: Sugar Free Pumpkin Spice Cookies

This cookie is especially popular with those people who love the fall season and all of the pumpkins spice everything that there is to eat and drink that one time of the year.

These cookies actually do have a bit of pumpkin added to them. However, they seem to resemble a sugar cookie in appearance, at least in my opinion. People seem to like how soft, chewy, and pumpkin tasting these cookies are because of the added pumpkin,

Here is what you will need to make this sugar free pumpkin spice cookies.

Flour (AP)- 2 1/2 cups.
Baking Soda- 1 teaspoon.
Baking Powder- 1 teaspoon.
Pumpkin Pie Spice– 1 teaspoon. (a substitute for this could be nutmeg+cinnamon).
Granular Sugar Alternative- 1 1/2 cups. For best results, use an alternative that measures 1:1 with sugar.
Butter- 10 tablespoons softened to room temperature.
Vanilla Extract- 1 teaspoon.
Canned Pumpkin- 1 cup (thats about 4-5 grams of natural sugar depending on the product).
Egg-1.

How To Make Sugar Free Pumpkin Spice Cookies
- *Preheat your oven to 325. Prep your cookie sheet for nonstick, parchment paper is my choice here.*
- *In a large bowl, whisk together the flour, baking soda, baking powder, pumpkin pie spice. Set this bowl aside.*
- *Next in a mixing bowl, cream together the sugar alternative and the butter*

- *.Add the vanilla, pumpkin, and egg to the mixing bowl and continue mixing.*
- *For the next step we will add the flour mixture from the first bowl to the mixing bowl. Do so adding by adding half of the mixture are time gently stirring between additions.*
- *Bake for 18-20 minutes or until these cookies appear to become firm.*
- *Remove the cookies from oven and allow them to sit on the cookie sheet for a few minutes before transferring to a rack.*

Read more at: https://thesugarfreediva.com/sugar-free-pumpkin-spice-cookies/

11: Sugar Free Lemon Drop Cookies

When I first saw sugar free lemon drops online I knew that there was a really good use for them. Well, I mean besides eating them out of the box. You can find out where to find sugar free lemon drop candy by following the link that at the end of this recipe.

I am a fan of most anything that has lemon in it. This cookie is no exception. I like how the tart flavor of lemon works with the sweet taste of the cookie.

Here is what you will need to make these lemon drop cookies.

Flour- 1 1/4 cups all purpose
Baking Powder- 1 teaspoon.
Crushed sugar free lemon drops- 1/3 cup
Lemon Zest- 1 1/2 teaspoons.
Butter- 1 stick plus 2 tablespoons softened at room temperature.
Sugar alternative- 3/4 cup, granular, Use an alternative that measures 1:1 with sugar.
Egg-1.
Cream (heavy,sour cream or an alternative such as Greek Yogurt)- 2 tablespoons.

How To Make Sugar Free Lemon Drop Cookies

- *Preheat your oven to 325 and prep your pan for nonstick. This is one case where I strongly recommend using parchment paper as melted candy can sometimes get a bit messy.*
- *In a medium sized bowl, mix together the flour, baking powder, crushed lemon drops and lemon zest. Set this bowl aside.*
- *Next, in a mixing bowl, use a paddle attachment and cream together the butter and sugar alternative.*
- *When the butter and sugar alternative are creamed, add the egg and the add the egg and then the cream to the mixing bowl and mix.*
- *Next, we will add the ingredients from the first bowl to this mixing bowl. Do this by adding half of the ingredients at a time, stirring between the addition.*

- *Use a spoon to drop the cookie dough onto the prepped pan allowing a bit of distance between cookies (about 1/2- 3/4").*
- *Bake these cookies for 10-12 minutes or until they appear to be browning.*
- *Allow the cookies to cool on the cookie sheet for a few minutes and then transfer to a cooling rack.*

Read more at: https://thesugarfreediva.com/sugar-free-lemon-drop-cookies/

12: Sugar Free Lemon Cookies

This cookie is a nice alternative to the regular basic tasting sugar cookie. It differs from many of my other cookie recipes because we are using a cake mix to make this cookie.

I am recommending a sugar free lemon cake mix (15-16 ounce package). However, if you cannot find a sugar free lemon cake you can easily use a white or angel sugar free cake mix with 1 lemon tablespoon of lemon zest added to it.

Here is what you will need to make this lemon cookie

Please note that this will recipe will yield more cookies than you may be use to baking in a batch of cookies.

Sugar Free Lemon Cake Mix- 1 box 15-16 ounces.
If you really are in a bind, try a white or angel sugar free cake mix with 1 lemon tablespoon of lemon zest added to it.
Lemon Zest-1 tablespoon.
Granular Sugar Alternative- 1 1/2 cups equivalent to sugar. Additional may be needed for coating the cookie for baking.
Eggs- 2. Vegetable
Vegetable Oil- 2/3 cups.
Lemon Extract- 1 teaspoon.
Vanilla Extract- 1 teaspoon.
Optional- topping such as powdered sugar or glaze (see post for details).

How To Make These Cookies.

- *Preheat your oven to 350 and prep a cookie pan for nonstick. I use parchment paper.*
- *Place your lemon cake mix into a mixing bowl.*
- *Next, beat in the eggs one at a time.*
- *Blend in the vegetable oil, lemon extract, and the vanilla extract with the other ingredients in the mixing bowl..*
- *Here is how to form your cookie for baking. If you are coating the cookies with sugar alternative prior to baking, you can skip to the net step. Note: this batter may seem to be a bit looser than a normal cookie batter. It will also bake to be a bit 'puffier' than a normal cookie as we are basing this recipe on a cake mix. Use a*

tablespoon to drop the cookies onto the cookie sheet rather than using a scoop or rolling them out
- *This next step is an optional step which is to coat the cookie with sugar free granular alternative prior to baking. The amount of alternative will depend upon your needs, 1/3rd cup of sugar alternative that measures 1:1 with sugar should be enough. Place the alternative into a shallow bowl and drip the cookie batter into the bowl and cover with sugar alternative. Then place the cookies onto the cookie sheet.*
- *Bake the cookies for 8-10 minutes. Cookies will be soft in the middle with slight browning on the sides/bottom when ready.*

Read more at: https://thesugarfreediva.com/easy-sugar-free-lemon-cookies/

13: 5 Ingredient Banana Oatmeal Cookies

This is the kind of a cookie is especially popular with moms who are looking for a cookie that is relatively healthy to feed their kids. While this cookie does not contain refined sugar, it does contain honey as the sweetener. You certainly could try making this with a honey alternative if you are not keen on the natural sugar that comes in honey.

What you will need to make this 5 ingredient banana oatmeal cookie recipe.

. Oats- 2 cups- quick oats.
Bananas- 3 ripened and mashed.
Peanut Butter- 3/4 cup (I have a recipe for sugar free peanut butter on my site).
Honey- 1 tablespoon.
Raisins (or chocolate chips) 1/4 cup.
Tip: I know someone who made this with just the first four ingredients to share with her pups!

How To Make This 5 Ingredient Banana Oatmeal Cookie Recipe.

- *Preheat your oven to 350. Prep your cookie tray with parchment paper or similar item.*
- *In a mixing bowl, combine together the oats and the mashed bananas.*
- *Next blend in the remaining ingredients and mix until well blended.*
- *Place the cookies on the prepped cookie tray using a tablespoon or other similar utensil. If the dough seems a bit too loose for you then you can add more oats as needed.*
- *Bake for 12-15 minutes or until the cookies begin to brown.*
- *Remove the cookies from the oven and allow to cool. 5 from 2 votes*

Read more at: https://thesugarfreediva.com/5-ingredient-banana-oatmeal-cookies/

14: 3 Ingredient Sugar Free Peanut Butter Cookies

This is another family friendly cookie idea. It has also been a popular recipe on my site. I like that there are only three ingredients in the great tasting cookies.

Here is what you will need to make this recipe.

Peanut Butter- 1 cup. Sugar free homemade or organic. I do have a recipe on thesugarfreediva.com for homemade sugar free peanut butter.

Sugar Alternative- 1 cup equivalent to sugar. For best results, use a sugar alternative that measures 1:1 with sugar. Splenda for baking is one example of this kind of a sugar alternative.

Egg- 1

Here Is How To Make These Cookies.

- *Preheat your oven to 325 degrees and prep your cookie sheet for nonstick. I like to use parchment paper for a recipe such as this one.*
- *In a large mixing bowl, combine together the peanut butter, sugar alternative and egg. Mix these ingredients until combined..*
- *Using a tablespoon, drop spoonfuls of cookie batter on to the prepped baking sheet. Leave at least 1/2" between cookie edges.*
- *Bake your cookies for 8-10 minutes or until appear to be set. Do not over-bake. These cookies are better when not burnt.*

Read more at: https://thesugarfreediva.com/3-ingredient-sugar-free-peanut-butter-cookies/

15: Sugar Free Lemon Shortbread Cookies

This delicious smelling and tasting recipe for Sugar Free Lemon Shortbread Cookies features two of my favorite things. I am a fan of both lemon anything and shortbread cookies.

I should also mention that this cookie is not only great for the December holiday season, it is also a popular one for Valentine's Day and Mother's Day.

What you will need to make this recipe.

Butter- 2 sticks + 1 tablespoon (1 cup + 1 tablespoon or 33 tablespoons) softened to room temperature.
Sugar Alternative– 3/4 cup. Please use a granular sugar alternative that measures 1:1 with sugar.
All Purpose Flour– 2 cups. See post for flour alternatives.
Lemon Zest– 1 teaspoon Vanilla Extract– 1 teaspoon

Here is how to make these cookies.

- *In a mixing bowl, beat together the butter with the sugar alternative. Then add the flour, lemon zest, and the vanilla extract to the bowl.*
- *Once the ingredients in the batter have been mixed you can divide it in half. Wrap each dough half in plastic wrap and refrigerate for at least thirty minutes.*
- *When you are ready to make your cookies remove the cookie dough from the refrigerator. Preheat your oven to 300 and prep your cookie sheets with parchment paper .*
- *We are going to roll out each of the cookie dough halves to cut into shapes. A great way to do this is to place a sheet of wax paper on a flat surface with one of the dough halves on top of it.*

Then place another sheet of wax paper over the dough that you just placed on top of the wax paper.
- *Using a rolling pin, roll out the dough (1/4-1/2") between the two sheets of wax paper.*
- *Bake the lemon shortbread cookies for 18-20 minutes or until they begin to brown on the edges. Allow the cookies to cool before topping them if desired.*

Read more at: https://thesugarfreediva.com/?p=7687

16: Sugar Free Graham Crackers

This recipe, which I would classify as a cookie as well as a cracker, is also a recipe for an essential ingredient for other recipes. If you have tried my sugar free s'more recipe then you know what I mean.

What you will need to make this recipe.

Graham Flour-1 cup
All purpose (AP) Flour- 1 cup.
Baking Powder- 1 teaspoon
Ground Cinnamon-1 teaspoon.
Sugar Alternative-1/4th cup of granular that measures 1:1 with sugar.
Butter- 1/2 Stick (1/4th cup) Softened.
Egg-1.
Molasses or alternative- 1/4th cup, honey can be used.
Vanilla Extract- 1 teaspoon.
Milk- 2 teaspoons.

How To Make This Recipe-

This recipe can actually be made in a food processor. Simply follow the standard instructions below in order to do so.

- *In a medium bowl, sift or whisk together the two flours, baking powder, and ground cinnamon.*
- *Next, in a mixing bowl, cream together the sugar alternative and the butter.*
- *Add the flour mixture from the first bowl to the mixing bowl, half at a time, mixing gently between addition. Then beat in your egg.*
- *Add the remaining ingredients (molasses or honey, vanilla extract, and milk) and mix until blended.*
- *Form a ball with your dough and then flatten it in plastic wrap. Fully cover the flattened ball of graham cracker dough and refrigerate it for at least thirty minutes.*
- *When you are ready to bake your graham crackers, remove the dough from the refrigerator.*

- *Preheat your oven to 350 and prep two baking sheet swith parchment paper.*
- *Divide the dough in half, one half per baking sheet. Roll the dough half out on the baking sheet to about 1/8th" width.*
- *When the dough has been rolled out, cut the crackers into squares and attempt to pull the sides away from one another while you cut.*
- *Optional- use a fork or similar item to make a design on each cracker. Also, you can sprinkle the tops with cinnamon and/or granular sugar alternative.*
- *Bake for 20-25 minutes or until the cracker edges begin to brown. Remove from oven and allow the graham crackers to cool on a rack.*

Read more at: https://thesugarfreediva.com/sugar-free-graham-crackers.

17: Sugar Free Low Carb Chocolate Turtles

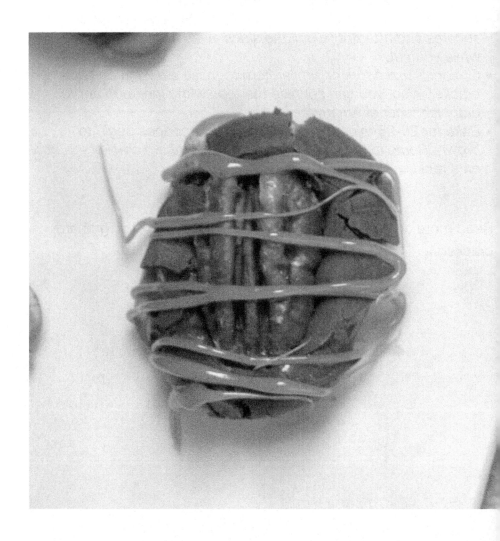

This recipe is for people like me who miss eating those yummy chocolate treats. Turtles combine the great tastes of chocolate, caramel and salty crunch. To be honest, this recipe could fall in both the candy and the cookie category depending on how you look at it. I will say that it chocolate turtles are a favorite holiday homemade treat for many.

For this recipe you will need to use sugar free caramels. To find sugar free caramels to use, please follow the link at the end of the recipe for details. Also, to make this low in carbs or keto, simply omit the pretzels,

What you will need to make this recipe.

Square Pretzels– 12-13 depending on number of caramels used and size of the pretzels. Most square pretzels have about 1 net carb in them. Omit this if you do not want that carb or if your pretzels's carb count is unsatisfactory for you.
Pecan Halves– 1 cup. Purchase toasted pecan halves or toast them yourself in a 320 oven for 5-7 minutes.
Sugar Free Chocolate Chips– 1 cup melted.
Water- 1 tablespoon.
Butter- 1/4 cup melted.
Sugar Free Caramels– 12-13 depending on size.

How To Make Sugar Free Low Carb Chocolate Turtles

- *Line a baking sheet or work space with parchment paper or buttered/ pre treated for nonstick foil.*
- *Arrange each pretzel on the prepared area from the last step, leaving ample room between the pretzels.*

- *Arrange the pecans on top of the pretzels that you have arranged on the prepared baking sheet.*
- *In a saucepan over medium-low heat, combine together the water, butter, and caramels.*
- *Slowly melt the ingredients in the saucepan together, stirring constantly. Then use a teaspoon to place a drop of the melted caramel over each prepared turtle.*
- *Allow this to cool a bit before proceeding. This is a good time to melt your chocolate.*
- *Use a spoon to drop melted chocolate over each of the turtles. When the chocolate has cooled you can drizzle additional caramel over the turtles and decorate as desired.*
- *Allow the turtles to set. You can refrigerate them once cooled to room temperature for at least an hour.*

Read more and find ingredients needed at: https://thesugarfreediva.com/sugar-free-low-carb-chocolate-turtles/

18: No Bake Sugar Free Chocolate Cookies

This recipe does not include eggs in it. Eggs are what are used in baked cookies to help keep the cookies together. Also missing from this recipe is flour of any kind.

I have a friend with small kids who love these cookies. She just makes them before they leave town and freezes them away to take with them.

What you will need to make these cookies.

Please note that you can find further information on how to find ingredients at the end of this recipe.

Granular Sugar Alternative- 1 1/2 cups. Please use a granular sugar alternative that measures 1:1 with sugar.
Milk- 1/2 cup. A nut based milk can be substituted in.
Butter- 1 stick (1/2 cup) Can use a butter alternative .
Unsweetened Cocoa Powder 1/4 cup.
Sugar Free Chocolate Chips– 1/4 cup.
Old Fashion Style of Rolled Oats– 3 cups.
Sugar Free Peanut Butter – 1 cup.
Vanilla Extract– 1 teaspoon.

HOW TO MAKE NO BAKE SUGAR FREE CHOCOLATE COOKIES

- *Start by prepping your cookie sheets with parchment or wax paper. Set this aside while you work.*
- *In a saucepan on medium heat, combine together sugar alternative, milk, butter, unsweetened cocoa powder, and sugar free chocolate chips. Bring this to a boil stirring as it heats. Be sure to scrape the sides of the pan to reduce sticking.*
- *Once the ingredients in the saucepan begin to bubble, wait one minute and then remove the pan from the heat.*

- *Stir in the remaining ingredients, one at a time. Then use a teaspoon to scoop the batter and drop it onto the prepped cookie sheet from the first step.*
- *This cookie should harden at room temperature within 45 minutes. Store the cookies in your refrigerator or freeze to take with you later on.*

Read more and learn about the ingredients at: https://thesugarfreediva.com/no-bake-sugar-free-chocolate-cookies/

19: Sugar Free Crinkle Cookies

This is another holiday cookie favorite. Thanks to my recipe for how to make sugar free powdered sugar, this cookie looks and tastes not unlike its original sugared counterpart. You can find the details about the ingredients in this recipe in the link following the recipe.

What you will need to make this crinkle cookie recipe

Flour- 1 2/3 cup (AP). Make this recipe gluten free by using gluten free flour instead of regular flour. Or, you can make this recipe low carb by using low carb Carbalose flour.
Unsweetened Cocoa Powder- 1/2 cup.
Baking Powder- 1 1/2 teaspoon.
Butter- 9 tablespoons (1 stick+ 1 tablespoon).
Sugar Alternative- 1 cup. Granular 1:1 equivalency with sugar works best.
Eggs- 2.
Vanilla Extract- 1 teaspoon.
Sugar Free Powdered Sugar 1/2 cup.

How to Make Sugar Free Crinkle Cookies

- *Mix together your flour, cocoa powder, and baking powder in a medium bowl. Set this aside.*
- *In a mixing bowl, blend together the butter and sugar alternative. When well blended, you can add the vanilla extract and then the eggs one at a time, stirring between additions.*
- *Next stir in the dry ingredients from the medium bowl to the mixing bowl. Be sure to scrape the sides of the bowl as needed to blend the ingredients together.*
- *Cover the cookie dough and refrigerate for at least 3 hours.*
- *When ready to bake the cookies, remove the mixing bowl from the refrigerator.*
- *Preheat the oven to 325 and prep your cookie sheets for nonstick. I like to use parchment paper*
- *Place your powdered sugar in a shallow bowl or similar surface.*
- *Use a tablespoon or similar sized scoop to scoop up cookie dough. Roll the dough into 1" balls and then roll each ball in the*

powdered sugar. Place each of the rolled cookie dough balls on the prepped sheet at least 2" apart.
- Bake for 12-14 minutes or until the cookies appear to be crackled and the outer areas of the cookies seem to be set.
- Allow your cookies to cool on a rack.

Read more and learn about the ingredients in this recipe at: https://thesugarfreediva.com/sugar-free-chocolate-crinkle-cookies/

20: Sugar Free Brownie Crackers

This is the perfect cookie for anyone looking for a cracker kind of crunch in their bite. That crunch comes from a brownie cookie that is flat like a cracker. What I like about this cookie is that it works great in other recipes or even as a sandwich with peanut butter in the center! Please see the link following this recipe for alternatives.

WHAT YOU WILL NEED TO MAKE THESE SUGAR FREE BROWNIE CRACKERS.

Flour– 1/3 cup.
Unsweetened Cocoa Powder– 1/4 cup.
Baking Soda– 1 teaspoon.
Butter- 1 stick (1/2 cup) melted.
Sugar alternative- equivalent to 1 cup of sugar. Please use a granular sugar alternative that also measures 1:1 with sugar for best results. Vanilla Extract– 1 teaspoon.
Egg White-1
Sugar Free Chocolate Chips – 1/2 cup

HOW TO MAKE THESE SUGAR FREE BROWNIE CRACKERS.

- *Start by preheating your oven to 325 degrees and prepping a cookie sheet for nonstick. I use parchment paper with a bit of nonstick spray on top for a recipe such as this one.*
- *In a medium bowl, mix together the flour, unsweetened cocoa powder and the baking soda. Set this bowl aside for a moment while you work.*
- *Next, in a mixing bowl, blend together the sugar alternative, vanilla extract and the egg white. Then stir in the the contents from the first bowl that you just had set aside.*
- *Transfer the mixture to your prepped cookie sheet, making sure to spread it as evenly as possible. A spatula or a scraper can help.*
- *Bake this for 15 minutes then cut it into squares without separating the pieces. Then press in the chocolate chips, as evenly dispersed as possible.*
- *Return to oven and bake for an additional 10 minutes. Remove from oven and allow to cool.*

Read more and learn about the ingredients at: https://thesugarfreediva.com/sugar-free-brownie-crackers/

21: Sugar Free Butter Cookies

Butter cookies are known for their distinctive butter taste. However, butter cookies are really quite a useful cookie in addition to being so tasty, Certainly, you can eat them as they are but, you can also drizzle some chocolate over them, cut them into fun shapes, or even make a cookie sandwich with them.

Here is what you will need to make these cookies.

Butter- 2 sticks (1 cup) softened to room temperature. Subbing in an alternative will take away from the 'butter taste' that is a part of this cookies.
Flour (AP)- 2 cups (see post for low carb alternatives).
Baking Powder- 1/4 tsp.
Salt- 1/2 tsp.
Sugar Alternative- I cup equivalent to sugar (1:1) granular alternative is recommended.
Egg-1.
Vanilla Extract-1 tsp.

How To Make Sugar Free Butter Cookies

- *Preheat your oven to 375.and line two cookie sheets with parchment paper for an easy clean-up.*
- *In a bowl, medium sized bowl, whisk together your flour, baking powder, and salt. Set this bowl aside.*
- *Next in a large mixing bowl, cream together the sugar alternative and the softened butter.*
- *For the next step, we will add the dry ingredients from the first bowl to the second (large mixing) bowl. Do this by adding half of the dry ingredients to the bowl, gently stirring, and then adding the rest.*
- *To the large mixing bowl, stir in the egg and vanilla extract.*

- *Optional: To prepare the cookie dough for using with cookie cutters, roll out the dough on a cookie sheet, cover with plastic, and refrigerate for at least 30 minutes to harden.*
- *Bake these cookies for 8-10 minutes or until the edges appear to start to brown.*

Read more at: https://thesugarfreediva.com/sugar-free-butter-cookies/

22: Sugar Free Crispy Cocoa Cookies

I developed this sugar free crispy cocoa cookie recipe after receiving several requests from readers. To be honest, I totally get that occasional craving to eat a crispy tasting cookie, like this one.

Here is what you will need to make this Crispy Cocoa Cookie recipe.

Flour (AP) – 1 cup (see original post for flour alternatives)
)Salt- 1 teaspoon.
Baking soda- 1/4 teaspoon.
Unsweetened Cocoa- 2 tablespoons.
Butter- 1 1/2 sticks (3/4 cup) room temperature softened.
Sugar alternative- equivalent to 1 1/2 cups of regular sugar.
Granular sugar alternative works best.
Egg- 1 large.
Vanilla Extract- 1 teaspoon.

How To Make Sugar Free Crispy Cocoa Cookies

- *Preheat your oven to 325 and prep your cookie sheet for nonstick. I am a fan of parchment paper. Also, get a cookie cooling rack ready to use.*
- *In a medium bowl, mix together the flour, salt, baking soda, and cocoa. Set this aside.*
- *Next, in a mixing bowl, cream together the butter, sugar alternative, egg, and vanilla extract.*
- *Add the dry mixture from the first bowl to the mixing bowl and continue to mix the ingredients. It is normal for this dough will appear to be thinner or wetter than a normal cookie dough. If the dough seems dry, add a bit of water or milk a teaspoon at a time (adding no more than 1/2 cup total).*
- *Scoop your cookies into balls and place on the cookie sheet. Then flatten the cookies with the palm of your hand. These cookies should be at least 1/2" apart.*
- *Bake your crispy cocoa cookies for 18-20 minutes or until they appear to be hardened., r*
- *Remove the cookies from oven and allow then to cool on the rack.*

- *This cookie dough can be made in advanced and refrigerated.*
- *Because of the consistency of the cookie, you may have better results if you refrigerate it after you have placed them as formed cookies on the cookie sheet.*

Read more at: https://thesugarfreediva.com/sugar-free-crispie-cocoa-cookies/

23: Sugar Free Gingerbread Cookies

I am sure that everyone reading this has some idea of what a gingerbread cookie is. This could be the most famous of holiday season cookies. We like to shape these cookies into fun shapes and sometimes put fun decorations and icing on top. As the name of this cookie suggests, this cookie is also about its ginger taste.

As a reminder, visiting the webpage listed at the end of this recipe will help you find ingredients that you may be looking for.

What you will need to make this sugar free ginger bread cookie.

Flour (AP)- 3 Cups
Baking Soda- 1 teaspoon.
Ground Ginger- 1 teaspoon (make sure there is no sugar added).
Ground Cinnamon- 1 teaspoon (make sure there is no sugar added). Ground cloves-1/2 teaspoon
Allspice- 1 teaspoon.
Salt- 1/2 teaspoon.
Butter- 1 1/2 sticks (3/4 cup) softened at room temperature.
Brown Sugar Alternative-1/2 cup
Egg-1
Molasses Substitute- 1 cup

HOW TO MAKE THESE COOKIES.

- *In a medium sized bowl, whisk or sift together the flour, baking soda, ground ginger, ground cinnamon, allspice and cloves. You can set this aside for a moment.*
- *Next, in a mixing bowl cream together the brown sugar alternative with the butter. Once it is creamed you can add the egg and then the molasses substitute.*

- *Now, gradually add your dry ingredient from the first bowl to the mixing bowl, a quarter at a time, mixing between additions.*
- *When the mixture is blended attempt to work it into a ball and then divide the dough in half.*
- *Working with one half of the dough at a time, roll out the dough on a flat surface that has been lightly floured. When the rolled out dough is about 1/4" to 1/8" thick you can wrap and refrigerate it for at least 3 hours.*
- *When ready to bake, simply remove the dough from the refrigerator, preheat your oven to 350, and prep your pan for nonstick. I use parchment that can also be used to transfer cookies as well.*
- *Working with one of the wrapped and refrigerated dough halves at a time, unwrap the dough on a work surface or parchment paper. Cut your cookies into desired shapes and place on the prepped sheets.*
- *Bake your cookies for 10-12 minutes or until they appear start browning on the edges.. After you remove the cookies from the oven please allow them to cool on rack before you add any icing.*

Read more at: https://thesugarfreediva.com/sugar-free-gingerbread-cookies-2/

24: Sugar Free Mexican Hot Chocolate Cookies

This recipe for Sugar Free Mexican Hot Chocolate Cookies features that famous taste that we expect from a cookie such as this one. Not only are we getting that great taste of a chocolate cookie with this, we are also getting a bit of spice to go with it.

Ingredients needed to make sugar free Mexican Hot Chocolate Cookies.

All Purpose Flour– 2 1/4 cups.
Unsweetened Cocoa Powder-1/2 cup.
Black Pepper– 1/2 teaspoon
Baking Soda–
Ground Cinnamon– 2 teaspoons, divided. Please use unsweetened cinnamon in this recipe.
Cayenne Pepper– 1 teaspoon
Cream of Tarter– 2 teaspoons.
Butter- 17 tablespoons, softened to room temperature. That is one cup + 1 tablespoon or 2 sticks + 1 tablespoon.
Granular Sugar Alternative– Equivalent to 1 1/2 cups of sugar, divided. Please use an alternative that measures the equivalent of 1:1 with sugar.
Eggs-2
Vanilla Extract– 1 teaspoon.
Sugar Free Chocolate Chips- 1 cup.

HOW TO MAKE SUGAR FREE MEXICAN HOT CHOCOLATE COOKIES

- *Preheat your oven to 350. Prep two cookie sheets for nonstick. I like to use Parchment Paper .*
- *In a medium sized bowl, whisk together the flour, Cocoa Powder, Black Pepper, Baking Soda, 1 teaspoon of Ground Cinnamon, Cayenne Pepper, and cream of tarter. Set this bowl aside.*

- *Next, in mixing bowl, cream together the butter with one cup of the sugar alternative.*
- *Once creamed, you can add the dry ingredients from the first bowl containing the dry ingredients (flour etc). To do so we will add half at a time, gently stirring between additions.*
- *Add the eggs one at a time, stirring gently between additions. And then the vanilla extract.*
- *Fold in the chocolate chips by hand. In a small bowl, use a fork to gently mix together the remaining sugar alternative and the remaining cinnamon.*
- *To form the cookies, use a tablespoon or similar item to scoop out dough. Form a ball with each ball of dough and then flatten it onto the prepped baking sheets. Sprinkle the remaining sugar alternative with cinnamon that is in the small bowl onto the cookies.*
- *Bake 12-15 minutes or until the cookies begin to crack. Allow to cool on the baking sheets.*

Read more at: https://thesugarfreediva.com/?p=7399

25: No Sugar Added Oatmeal And Raisin Cookies

This chewy and soft recipe for no sugar added oatmeal and raisin cookies is so delicious! I like that the oatmeal and raisins are healthy ingredients to add to this recipe.

Please refer to the webpage link that follows this recipe for ingredient information.

WHAT YOU WILL NEED TO MAKE THIS NO SUGAR ADDED OATMEAL AND RAISIN COOKIES

All Purpose Flour– 1 1/2 cups.
Granular Sugar Alternative– equivalent to 3/4 cup of sugar. Please use a granular sugar alternative that measures 1:1 with sugar.
Brown Sugar Alternatives – Equivalent to 1/2 cup of brown sugar.
Butter- 1 cup (2 sticks) softened to room temperature
Vanilla Extract– 1 teaspoon.
Eggs-2.
Rolled Oats– 3 cups
Raisins – 1 cup.

HOW TO MAKE NO SUGAR ADDED OATMEAL AND RAISIN COOKIES

- *Preheat your oven to 350 and prep your cookie sheets for nonstick. I like to use Parchment Paper .*
- *In a medium bowl, whisk together the flour, baking soda, and ground cinnamon. Set this bowl aside.*
- *Now in a mixing bowl, cream together the granular sugar alternative and the butter. Then add the vanilla and the eggs, gently stirring them into the mixing bowl.*
- *For the next step, we will add the dry ingredients from the first bowl (flour etc) to the mixing bowl. Do this by adding half of the dry ingredients at a time, mixing gently between additions. Then continue mixing the cookie dough until the ingredients are mixed together. Next, stir in the oatmeal and raisins by hand.*

- *Bake these cookies for 10-12 minutes or until the edges begin to brown.*

Read more at: https://thesugarfreediva.com/?p=2541

26: Sugar Free Flour Free Chocolate Chip Cookies

Chocolate chip cookies are probably the most popular cookie among cookie lovers everywhere. There is no wonder why since these cookies feature everything that is good in a cookie from chocolate to a buttery taste. This is just one of my many different ways to bake up that chocolate chip cookie without adding sugar to it.

For ingredient details, please refer to the webpage listed at the end of this recipe.

HERE IS WHAT YOU WILL NEED TO MAKE THIS SUGAR FREE FLOUR FREE CHOCOLATE CHIP COOKIES

Sugar Free Peanut Butter– 1 cup
Sugar Alternative– 3/4 cup. Please use a granular sugar alternative that measures 1:1 with sugar.
Baking Soda– 1 teaspoon.
Vanilla Extract– 1 teaspoon
Egg-1
Sugar Free Chocolate Chips- 1 cup
Kosher Salt– 3 teaspoons or as desired. This is optional and for dusting the tops of the cookie very lightly. If you are using a salty butter you may not even need the salt dusting.

HOW TO MAKE SUGAR FREE FLOUR FREE CHOCOLATE CHIP COOKIES

- *Preheat your oven to 325 and line two baking sheets with parchment paper.*
- *In a medium to large bowl, blend together the peanut butter with the sugar alternative. Then stir int the baking soda, vanilla extract and the egg. Follow this by folding in the chocolate chips.*
- *Use a scoop or tablespoon to drop the cookie dough onto the prepped baking sheets. Be sure to leave room between cookies for them to spread.*
- *Dust with the Kosher Salt.*

- *Bake your cookies for 12-14 minutes or until done. Keep in mind that how you bake these cookies can determine how they will turn out. That is, if you bake this cookie until the edges start to turn brown and then transfer the cookie to a rack to cool, your cookie will result in a softer texture. On the other hand, allowing your cookie to brown a bit more and cool on the warm cookie sheet, you will have a more crisp result from this recipe.*

Read more at: https://thesugarfreediva.com/?p=7412

27: Sugar Free Ginger Snap Cookies

As you probably already know, ginger snap cookies are a standard cookie to eat during the holiday season. The ginger snap cookies is known for its blended seasonings of both the fall and holiday seasons. I am referring to the ground ginger (hence the 'ginger' in the name) and the cinnamon that go into these yummy cookies.

WHAT YOU WILL NEED TO MAKE SUGAR FREE GINGER SNAP COOKIES

Flour (AP)– 2 cups.
Ground Cinnamon– 1 teaspoon.
Ground Ginger– 2 teaspoons.
Baking Soda– 1 teaspoon.
Butter- 3/4 cup + 1 tablespoon (1 1/2 sticks + 1 tablespoon), softened to room temperature.
Granular Sugar Alternative– 1 cup. Please use one that measures 1:1 with sugar in volume.
Egg-1.
Molasses– 1/2 cup, dark is preferred. Please refer to the webpage listed at the end of this recipe for alternatives to molasses that you can use in this recipe.

HOW TO MAKE SUGAR FREE GINGER SNAP COOKIES

- *Preheat your oven to 325 and prep a cookie sheet for nonstick. I like to use Parchment Paper .*
- *In a medium bowl, sift together the flour, cinnamon, ginger, and baking soda. Set this bowl aside.*
- *Next, cream together the sugar alternative in a large mixing bowl. Once it is creamed, you can beat in the molasses and the egg.*
- *For the next step, we are going to add the contents from the first bowl with the dry ingredients (flour etc) to the large mixing bowl. Do this by adding half of the dry ingredients, mix gently and then add the remaining ingredients.*
- *Roll the cookies into balls and place onto the cookie sheet, far enough apart to allow from spreading as they bake. You can roll*

the cookies in additional granular sugar alternative if desired prior to placing onto the cookie sheet.
- *Bake the cookies for 10-12 minutes or until they begin to 'crack'.*

Read more at: https://thesugarfreediva.com/?p=7231

28: Sugar Free Soft Pumpkin Cookies

What I like about this cookie, besides of course the pumpkin in them, is that these cookies are made in an 'old time' style kind of like what you would expect from grandmas kitchen. You will see what I mean when you see these cookies for yourself.

Please refer to the webpage listed at the end of this recipe for further ingredient information.

WHAT YOU WILL NEED TO MAKE THIS SUGAR FREE SOFT PUMPKIN COOKIES

Pumpkin puree comes in a can (usually 15 ounce) and is the kind of pumpkin that is used in baking recipes such as this one.

Flour (AP) – 2 1/2 cups.
Baking Soda– 1 1/2 teaspoons.
Baking Powder– 1/2 teaspoon.
Ground Cinnamon– 1 teaspoon.
Ground Nutmeg– 1 teaspoon.
Granulated Sugar Alternative– 1 1/4 cup. Please use a granulated sugar alternative that measures 1:1 with sugar for best results.
Butter- 9 tablespoons softened to room temperature. That is one stick + 1 tablespoon or 1/2 cup plus one tablespoon.
Pumpkin Puree – 1 cup.
Egg-1.
Vanilla Extract– 1 teaspoon.

HOW TO MAKE SUGAR FREE SOFT PUMPKIN COOKIES

- *Preheat your oven to 325 and prep your cookie sheets for nonstick. I like to use Parchment Paper .*
- *In a medium bowl, whisk together the flour, baking soda, baking powder, ground cinnamon, and ground nutmeg. Set this bowl aside. Next, in a mixing bowl, cream together the sugar*

alternative with the butter. Once this is blended, you can beat in the pumpkin puree and then the vanilla extract and egg.
- *For this next step, we will add the flour mixture from the medium bowl to the mixing bowl. To do so add half of the mixture at a time gently mixing between the additions.*
- *Bake your cookies for 18-20 minutes or until the cookies appear to start browning and firming.*
- *Allow the cookies to cool before adding a glaze. Alternatively, sprinkle with granulate sugar alternative about 12 minutes into baking to get more of a sugar cookie style to this cookie.*

Read more at: https://thesugarfreediva.com/?p=7395

29: Sugar Free Mexican Wedding Cookies

In case you are wondering, this is a very popular cookie to eat in Mexico. These cookies are known as a polvorones in Mexico and are especially popular during the holiday season. You may also be wondering if Mexican Wedding Cookies are the same thing as

Snowballs or Russian Tea Cakes. To the eye, these cookies all look the same, they are round and covered in powdered sugar.

Unlike many cookies, this one does not include baking soda or a similar ingredient.
Please refer to the webpage listed at the end of this recipe for ingredient details and how to find them.

WHAT INGREDIENTS YOU WILL NEED TO MAKE THESE SUGAR FREE MEXICAN WEDDING COOKIES

Butter- 1 cup + 1 tablespoon (17 tablespoons total) softened to room temperature.
Granular Sugar Alternative- 1/2 cup equivalent to sugar. Please use a granular sugar alternative that measures 1:1 with sugar.
Vanilla Extract– 2 teaspoons.
Flour (AP)– 1 3/4 cups.
Nuts- 1 cup chopped. I like a pecan nuts in this recipe. However, almonds or walnuts or even a combination of these choices are all good tasting bets in this cookie.
Sugar Free Powdered Sugar- 1/2-3/4 cup.

HOW TO MAKE SUGAR FREE MEXICAN WEDDING COOKIES

- *This is a cookie dough that can be made in advance and refrigerated for later baking.*
- *If you are baking these cookies now, preheat your oven to 300 and line your cookie sheets with parchment paper.*
- *Start by creaming together the softened butter with the granular sugar alternative at a low speed in a mixing bowl. Then blend in the vanilla extract.*

- *Next, we will add the flour to the mixing bowl. It is best to do this by adding half of the flour at a time, mixing gently between additions.*
- *Then you can fold in the chopped nuts.*
- *For this next step we will shape the cookies into balls (or other shape such as crescent) and place the cookies onto the prepared cookie sheets. Tip: use a tablespoon to scoop out the cookie dough to make your cookie size consistent. Also, if your cookie dough seems to be a bit sticky, you can coat your hands with a bit of flour or oil.*
- *Bake for 18-20 minutes and allow to cool on a cookie rack, When cooled, roll the cookies in the powdered sugar to coat them.*

Read more at: https://thesugarfreediva.com/?p=7420

30: Sugar Free Peanut Butter Blossom Cookies

There are many different names for this cookie including ones that include famous 'kiss inspired' chocolate candy in them. Since sugar free chocolate 'kiss inspired' candy does not exist (as to my knowledge at this time) you will either need to make your own or simply substitute in another kind of sugar free candy or chocolate chips.

For details on how to make your own sugar free chocolate 'kiss inspired' candy or other ingredient details, please refer to the webpage listed at the end of this recipe.

WHAT YOU WILL NEED TO MAKE THIS SUGAR FREE PEANUT BUTTER BLOSSOM COOKIES

All Purpose Flour– 1 1/2 cups.
Baking Soda– 1/2 teaspoon.
Baking Powder– 1/2 teaspoon.
Butter- 1/2 cup (1 stick) softened to room temperature
Sugar Alternative (granulated)– 3/4 cup equivalent to regular sugar. Please use a granular sugar alternative that measures 1:1 with sugar. Granular Brown Sugar Alternative– 1/4 cup. Again, please use a granular brown sugar alternative that measures like regular brown sugar Sugar Free Peanut Butter– 3/4 cup.
Egg-1.
Vanilla Extract- 1 teaspoon.
Sugar Free Chocolate Candy- 36 ('kiss inspired') or as needed.

HOW TO MAKE SUGAR FREE PEANUT BUTTER BLOSSOM COOKIES

- *Preheat your oven to 350 and prep your cookies sheets as needed. I like to use Parchment Paper .*
- *In a medium bowl, whisk together the flour, baking soda and baking powder. Set this bowl aside for a moment.*
- *Next, in a mixing bowl and low to medium speed, cream together your sugars (white and brown) with your butter and peanut butter. Then beat in the egg and vanilla extract.*
- *For the next step, we will add the dry ingredients from the first bowl to the mixing bowl. Do this by adding half of the dry ingredients at a time, stirring between additions.*

- *To form the cookies, simply use a tablespoon to measure out the dough needed for each cookie. Roll the dough into a ball.*
- *If desired, you can roll the ball in additional granular sugar alternative, and then place the balls on to the cookie sheet. Do not press the balls flat and also be sure to leave plenty of room between the balls as the cookies will spread while baking.*
- *Bake your cookies for 10-12 minutes or until the edges begin to brown.*
- *Remove from the oven and press the chocolate candy into the center of the cookie before the cookie can cool.*

Read more at: https://thesugarfreediva.com/?p=7424

31: Sugar Free Chocolate Chocolate Chip Cookies

If you like chocolate with chocolate and you like cookies then you will probably really like this recipe for Sugar Free Chocolate

Chocolate Chip Cookies. This is especially true if you are wanting to not have a lot of sugar in that great tasting cookie!

WHAT YOU WILL NEED TO MAKE THIS SUGAR FREE CHOCOLATE CHOCOLATE CHIP COOKIES

Flour (AP)– 2 cups.
Baking Powder– 3/4 teaspoon.
Baking Soda-1/2 teaspoon.
Unsweetened Cocoa Powder– 1/2 cup.
Butter- 1 cup+ 1 tablespoon (17 tablespoons total) softened to room temperature. You can sub in margarine or a butter flavored shortening for half of the butter in this recipe to make a softer cookie.
Granular Sugar Alternative – 1 1/4 cups equivalent to sugar. that measures 1:1 with sugar. Please use a granular sugar alternative that measures 1:1 with sugar for best results.
Eggs- 2.
Vanilla Extract– 2 teaspoons.
Sugar Free Chocolate Chips 1 1/2 cups

HOW TO MAKE SUGAR FREE CHOCOLATE CHOCOLATE CHIP COOKIES

- *Preheat your oven to 325 and line a baking sheet with parchment paper .*
- *In a medium bowl, whisk together the flour, baking powder, baking soda, and unsweetened cocoa powder. Set this bowl aside while you continue.*
- *In a mixing bowl, cream together your butter with your sugar alternative. Then and the eggs and the vanilla and beat until somewhat fluffy.*

- *For the next step, we will add the dry ingredients from the first bowl to the mixing bowl. Do this by adding half of the dry ingredients at a time, stirring between additions taking care to not over mix your cookie dough. Then, fold in your chocolate chips.*
- *Bake your cookies for 10-12 minutes or until they appear to be set. Cool these cookies on a wire rack.*

Read more at: https://thesugarfreediva.com/?p=7432

32: Sugar Free Peanut Butter Buckeye Balls

An ode to the Buckeye tree nuts in Ohio, these Sugar Free Peanut Butter Buckeye Balls are such a yummy treat. I love the way that the chocolate and peanut butter work together in creating such as delicious taste. This is a popular addition to any holiday dessert spread.

Please refer to the webpage listed after the recipe for ingredient details.

What you will need to make this recipe for Sugar Free Buckeyes

Sugar Free Peanut Butter– 1 1/2 cups.
Butter- 1 cup softened to just about melted. This is equivalent to two sticks of butter.
Sugar Free Powdered Sugar– 6 cups.
Vanilla Extract– 1 teaspoon.
Sugar Free Chocolate Chips – 4 cups.

How to make this recipe.

We will first make the peanut butter balls and then allow them to freeze. After the balls have hardened, we will dip them into melted chocolate. This recipe works well when the balls are placed on wax paper.

- *Prepare a baking sheet, with wax paper and set this aside.*
- *In a mixing bowl, cream together the sugar free peanut butter, butter, sugar free powdered sugar and vanilla extract.*
- *When you are able to, form the mixture into individual 1- 1 1/2" balls by rolling the dough between your hands.*
- *Place each ball on the wax papered baking sheet. Tip: place a toothpick into each of the balls to make dipping easier later on.*

- *Place the prepared balls in the freezer until hard- about 25-35 minutes.*
- *When you are ready to dip the balls in the chocolate, melt the chocolate in a microwave or using the double boiler method. Be sure to stir well as the chocolate melts. If using a microwave, simply microwave for 30 second intervals stirring between intervals. You want the chocolate to be really very warm for best results in this recipe.*
- *Remove the peanut butter balls from the freezer and dip each one into the chocolate, leaving the area around the toothpick free of chocolate. Then place the individual balls back on to the wax paper and refrigerate them. If you run low on chocolate simply melt more.*

Read more at: https://thesugarfreediva.com/?p=7438

Final Thoughts

These recipes in this sugar free holiday cookie recipe books are intended to give you some inspiration in your holiday baking efforts.

Because we are using alternatives to sugar, many adjustments may need to be made in the recipes. Sometimes, there may be some trial and error as well.

For updates to recipes and to learn more about alternatives and tips in the specific recipe, please refer to the webpage listed at the end of each specific recipe for details.

Learn more about my Guide to Sugar Free Baking and other recipe books on amazon. https://amzn.to/2B73sSt

Thank you for the following!

Thesugarfreediva.com | @thesugarfreediva | pinterest.com/thesugarfreediva/ | facebook.com/thesugarfreediva/ | instagram.com/thesugarfreediva/

Made in the USA
Coppell, TX
01 May 2021

54808536R00066